T0220237

JavaScript Quick
Syntax Reference

■ ■ ■

Mikael Olsson

Apress®

JavaScript Quick Syntax Reference

ISBN-13 (pbk): 978-1-4302-6493-4

ISBN-13 (electronic): 978-1-4302-6494-1

Managing Director: Welmoed Spahr
Lead Editor: Steve Anglin
Technical Reviewer: Victor Sumner
Editorial Board: Steve Anglin, Mark Beckner, Louise Corrigan, Jonathan Gennick,
    Robert Hutchinson, Michelle Lowman, James Markham, Susan McDermott,
    Matthew Moodie, Jeffrey Pepper, Douglas Pundick, Ben Renow-Clarke,
    Gwenan Spearing, Steve Weiss
Coordinating Editor: Mark Powers
Copy Editor: Karen Jameson
Compositor: SPi Global
Indexer: SPi Global
Artist: SPi Global

Distributed to the book trade worldwide by Springer Science+Business Media New York, 233 Spring Street, 6th Floor, New York, NY 10013. Phone 1-800-SPRINGER, fax (201) 348-4505, e-mail orders-ny@springer-sbm.com, or visit www.springeronline.com. Apress Media, LLC is a California LLC and the sole member (owner) is Springer Science + Business Media Finance Inc (SSBM Finance Inc). SSBM Finance Inc is a **Delaware** corporation.

For information on translations, please e-mail rights@apress.com, or visit www.apress.com.

Apress and friends of ED books may be purchased in bulk for academic, corporate, or promotional use. eBook versions and licenses are also available for most titles. For more information, reference our Special Bulk Sales–eBook Licensing web page at www.apress.com/bulk-sales.

Any source code or other supplementary material referenced by the author in this text is available to readers at www.apress.com/9781430264934. For detailed information about how to locate your book's source code, go to www.apress.com/source-code/. Readers can also access source code at SpringerLink in the Supplementary Material section for each chapter.

Contents at a Glance

Contents

About the Author

Mikael Olsson is a professional web entrepreneur, programmer, and author. He works for an R&D company in Finland where he specializes in software development. In his spare time he writes books and creates web sites that summarize various fields of interest. The books he writes are focused on teaching their subject in the most efficient way possible, by explaining only what is relevant and practical without any unnecessary repetition or theory. The portal to his online businesses and other websites is Siforia.com.

About the Technical Reviewer

Victor Sumner is a senior software engineer at D2L Corporation, where he helps to build and maintain an integrated learning platform. As a self-taught developer, he is always interested in emerging technologies and enjoys working on and solving problems that are outside his comfort zone. When not at the office, Victor has a number of hobbies, including photography, horseback riding, and gaming. He lives in Ontario, Canada, with his wife, Alicia, and their two children.

Introduction

JavaScript is a programming language primarily used as a client-side scripting language for controlling how web sites behave. In this environment the language complements HTML, which describes the structure of web documents; and CSS, the style language that defines their appearance. When embedded on a web page, JavaScript allows the page to execute code and respond dynamically to user actions, providing responsiveness and interactivity in a way not achievable using only HTML.

As the de facto client-side scripting language for the Web, most every browser includes an engine for running JavaScript source code. Historically, these engines ran JavaScript code line by line without preliminary compilation, so-called interpretation. Nowadays modern browsers perform just-in-time (JIT) compilation, which compiles JavaScript to executable bytecode just as it is about to run. This has significantly improved the performance of JavaScript, enabling the development of fast web applications, such as Gmail, that blurs the line between web sites and desktop applications.

The JavaScript language was created in 1995 by Brendan Eich at Netscape under the name Mocha. It was later renamed to LiveScript and finally to JavaScript within the same year. Netscape Navigator 2 was the first browser to implement JavaScript in 1996. That same year Microsoft released a compatible language for Internet Explorer 3, which was called JScript for trademark reasons. To maintain compatibility across browsers, Netscape had the language standardized by Ecma International under the name ECMAScript.

The name JavaScript is derived from the Java programming language, as a marketing ploy by Netscape to capitalize on the popularity of Java. Netscape wanted a simple, interpreted language that would be easier than Java for nonprofessional programmers to use on the Web. JavaScript borrows much of its syntax from Java, and the languages are both object oriented, but they are still two very different languages. In contrast to Java, JavaScript code does not need to be compiled, and it cannot produce stand-alone applications.

As a scripting language, JavaScript is designed to run in a host environment, where the host provides mechanisms for communicating with the outside world. The most common host environment is the web browser, but JavaScript engines can also be found in many other environments, such as desktops, databases, embedded systems, and server-side environments. This book will focus exclusively on the browser environment since this remains the dominant place in which JavaScript is used.

CHAPTER 1

■ ■ ■

Using JavaScript

To begin experimenting with JavaScript, you should install an Integrated Development Environment (IDE) that supports this language. There are many good choices, such as NetBeans, Eclipse, Visual Studio, and Brackets. In this book we will be using NetBeans, which is available for free from Netbeans.org.[1] To follow along make sure you download one of the bundles that include HTML 5 support, as this also includes support for JavaScript.

Alternatively, you can develop using a simple text editor – such as Notepad – although this is less convenient than using an IDE. If you choose to do so, just create an empty document with an .html file extension and open it in the editor of your choice.

Creating a Project

After installing NetBeans, go ahead and launch the program. You then need to create a project, which will manage the HTML source files and other resources of your website. Go to File ➤ New Project to display the New Project window. From there select the HTML 5 category in the left frame, and then the HTML 5 Application project in the right frame. Click the Next button and you can configure the name and location of the project. When you are done, click Finish to let the wizard make your project.

You have now created an HTML 5 project. In the Projects panel (Window ➤ Projects) you can see that the project consists of a single file called index.html, located in your site's root folder. The file contains some basic HTML 5 markup, which can be simplified further to the markup seen below.

```
<!doctype html>
<html>
 <head><title>JavaScript Test</title></head>
 <body></body>
</html>
```

---

[1]https://netbeans.org/downloads/.

Embedding JavaScript

There are two ways of inserting JavaScript into a web document. The first is to place the code within a `script` element. A document can have multiple such elements, and each can enclose any number of JavaScript statements.

```
<script></script>
```

The other, more common method is to include the code in an external file and then link to that file using the `src` attribute of the `script` element. This way several documents can use the same code without having to duplicate it on every page.

```
<script src="mycode.js"></script>
```

By convention, the `.js` extension is used for files that contain JavaScript code. To add a new file with this name to your NetBeans project, right-click on the Site Root folder in the Projects panel and select New ➤ JavaScript file. From the dialog box give the source file the name "mycode.js." Click Finish and the file will be added to your project and opened for you.

For the purpose of experimentation, you can inline your code using the first method of embedding. However, for real world applications, all but the simplest of scripts should be made external. This makes the code easier to read and maintain, as it separates the JavaScript code (page behavior) from the HTML markup (page content). As external files are cached by browsers, this also improves performance of the site.

Displaying Text

As is common when learning a new programming language, the first example JavaScript code will display a "Hello World" text string. This is accomplished by adding the following line within the body element of the web document.

```
<script>
  document.write("Hello World");
</script>
```

This code statement uses the `write` method that belongs to the `document` object. The method accepts text as its argument, delimited by double quotes. These concepts will be explored further in later chapters.

Statements in JavaScript are separated by semicolons. The semicolon may be omitted if the statement is followed by a line break, as this is also interpreted as a statement separator.

```
document.write("Hello World")
```

The full web document should now look like this.

```
<!doctype html>
<html>
 <head><title>JavaScript Test</title></head>
 <body>
 <script>
  document.write("Hello World");
 </script>
 </body>
</html>
```

To view the page, open the HTML file with a web browser. In NetBeans, this is done by clicking Run ➤ Run Project (F6), or by clicking the green arrow on the toolbar. You can select your preferred browser from Run ➤ Set Project Browser. When the document is viewed in the browser, the script is executed as soon as the page loads and the text string is displayed.

View Source

While you have the browser opened, you can view the source code that makes up the page by pressing Ctrl + U. This shortcut works in all major browsers, including Chrome, Firefox, and Internet Explorer (IE). The source code window reveals the HTML markup, as well as the unparsed JavaScript code.

Viewing the source code of web pages in this way provides a great way to learn from other web developers. Whenever you find an interesting feature on a web page – whether it is made with HTML, CSS, JavaScript or another language – the page source will often reveal how it was created.

Browser Compatibility

JavaScript is most often run on the client-side, inside the browser, as opposed to the server-side. For the code to be executed it is therefore required that the client views the document in a browser that supports JavaScript.

Since JavaScript is the most popular client-side scripting language, it works with virtually all browsers in use today. However, the client may choose to disable JavaScript, so there is no way to guarantee that client-side code is executed. Even so, most web sites today use JavaScript, and many rely on it to function correctly.

HTML provides the noscript element to specify alternative content for browsers that do not support JavaScript or that have it disabled.

```
<noscript>
Please enable JavaScript for full functionality of this site.
</noscript>
```

Console Window

Most browsers have a development console available that allows you to view information from your JavaScript code for debugging purposes. To print information to this console, the log method of the console object is used.

```
<script>
  console.log("Hello Console");
</script>
```

The process for bringing up the console is the same in Chrome, Firefox, and Internet Explorer. You right-click on the page and select Inspect Element. This brings up the development window from where you can find the Console tab. In Internet Explorer, you will need to launch the development window first and then refresh the page in order to view the console output.

Comments

Comments are used to clarify code to developers and they have no effect on the parsing of the code. JavaScript has the standard notations for single-line (//) and multiline (/**/) comments, as used by many other languages.

```
<script>
  // single-line comment
  /* multi-line
     comment */
</script>
```

As in HTML, whitespace characters – such as spaces, tabs, and comments – are generally ignored in JavaScript. This allows you a lot of freedom in how to format your code. The formatting you use is a matter of preference. Choose a style that makes sense to you and aim to keep it consistent.

Code Hints

If you are unsure of what a specific object contains, or what arguments a function takes, you can take advantage of code hints in some IDEs, such as NetBeans. The code hint window is brought up by pressing Ctrl + Space and provides quick access to any code entities you are able to use within the current context. This is a powerful feature that you should learn to make good use of.

CHAPTER 2

Variables

Variables are containers used for storing data, such as numbers or strings, so that they can be used multiple times in a script.

Declaring Variables

To create a variable the var keyword is used followed by a name, called the identifier. A common naming convention for variables is to have each word initially capitalized, except for the first one.

```
var myVar;
```

A value can be assigned to a variable by using the equals sign, which is called the assignment operator (=). This is called assigning or initializing the variable.

```
myVar = 10;
```

The declaration and assignment can be combined into a single statement. When a variable is assigned a value it then becomes defined.

```
var myVar = 10;
```

There is a shorthand way of creating multiple variables in the same statement by using the comma operator (,).

```
var myVar = 10, myVar2 = 20, myVar3;
```

Once a variable has been declared, it can be used by referencing the variable's name. For example, the value of a variable can be printed to a web document by passing the identifier to the document.write method.

```
document.write(myVar); // "10"
```

Keep in mind that variable identifiers are case sensitive, so uppercase and lowercase letters have different meanings. Identifiers in JavaScript can include letters, dollar signs ($), underscore characters (_), and numbers, but they cannot start with a number. They also cannot contain spaces or special characters, and must not be a reserved keyword.

```
var _myVar32; // allowed
var 32Var;    // incorrect (starts with number)
var my Var;   // incorrect (contains space)
var var@32;   // incorrect (contains special character)
var var;      // incorrect (reserved keyword)
```

Dynamic Typing

JavaScript is a dynamically typed language. Therefore, the data type of a variable does not need to be specified, and any variable can hold any data type.

```
var myType = "Hi"; // string type
myType = 1.5;      // number type
```

Furthermore, the value of a variable will be converted automatically as needed, depending on the context in which it is used.

```
// Number type evaluated as string type
console.log(myType); // "1.5"
```

Because of these implicit type conversions, knowing the underlying type of a variable is not always necessary. Nevertheless, it is useful to know about the data types JavaScript works with in the background. These six types are as follows: Number, Bool, String, Object, Undefined, and Null.

Number Type

JavaScript has a single type for both integer and floating-point numbers. Integers can be expressed by using decimal (base 10), octal (base 8), or hexadecimal (base 16) notation. A leading zero on an integer value indicates it is octal, and a leading 0x (or 0X) indicates hexadecimal. Hexadecimal integers can include digits 0-9 and letters A-F, while octal integers can include only the digits 0-7. The following integer literals all represent the same number, which in decimal notation is 10.

```
var dec = 10;  // decimal notation
var oct = 012; // octal notation
var hex = 0xA; // hexadecimal notation
```

Floating-point numbers can be represented with either decimal or exponential (scientific) notation. The exponential notation is used by adding E (or e) followed by the decimal exponent.

```
var num = 1.23;
var exp = 3e2; // 3*10^2 = 300
```

Keep in mind that all numbers in JavaScript are stored as double-precision floating-point numbers behind the scenes.

Bool Type

The bool type can store a Boolean value, which is a value that can only be either true or false. These values are specified with the true and false keywords.

```
var myBool = true;
```

Boolean values are commonly used together with conditional and looping statements, which will be looked at in later chapters.

Undefined Type

JavaScript has a value called undefined that is used to indicate the absence of a value. This is the value a declared variable receives if it is not given an initial value.

```
var myUndefined;
console.log(myUndefined); // "undefined"
```

The data type used for storing this value is also named undefined. This can be shown by using the typeof operator, which retrieves a string representation of a type.

```
console.log(typeof myUndefined); // "undefined"
```

Bear in mind that an undefined variable is not the same as an undeclared variable. Any attempt to access an undeclared variable will result in a ReferenceError exception being thrown, halting execution of the script.

```
console.log(myUndeclared); // throws a ReferenceError
```

Null Type

The type and value null represents an object with no value. In contrast to undefined, which can result from language-level behavior, the value null is always set through code. It is often used as a function return value that indicates an exception or error condition.

```
var myNull = null;
console.log(myNull); // "null"
```

Although null is a data type, the typeof operator will evaluate this type as an object. This is considered to be a mistake in the language specification.

```
console.log(typeof myNull); // "object"
```

In Boolean contexts both null and undefined are evaluated as false. The following example uses the not operator (!) to coerce these values to the Boolean type. This operator inverts a Boolean result and is therefore used twice to retrieve the original value's Boolean representation.

```
console.log(!!null);      // "false"
console.log(!!undefined); // "false"
```

Conversely, in numeric contexts null behaves as 0 while undefined causes the whole expression to evaluate as NaN.

```
console.log(null * 5);      // "0"
console.log(undefined * 5); // "NaN"
```

Special Numeric Values

JavaScript has three special numeric values: Infinity, -Infinity, and NaN. These values are used to signal that some exception happened during a calculation. For instance, the following calculations result in these three values.

```
console.log(1 / 0);  // "Infinity"
console.log(-1 / 0); // "-Infinity"
console.log(0 / 0);  // "NaN"
```

The value NaN is short for Not-A-Number and denotes an unrepresentable numeric value. It is the return value typically used when math operations fail. For instance, taking the square root out of -1 results in NaN. This calculation can be performed using the sqrt method of the global Math object.

```
var myNaN = Math.sqrt(-1);
console.log(myNaN);        // "NaN"
console.log(typeof myNaN); // "number"
```

Attempting to evaluate a non-numeric value in a numeric context will also result in NaN.

```
console.log("Hi" * 3); // "NaN"
```

NaN has the odd property of comparing unequally to any other value, including another NaN value. To determine whether a value is NaN, the global isNaN function can be used.

```
console.log(NaN == NaN);   // "false"
console.log(isNaN(myNaN)); // "true"
```

CHAPTER 3

Operators

An operator is a symbol that makes the script perform a specific mathematical or logical manipulation. The operators in JavaScript can be grouped into five types: arithmetic, assignment, comparison, logical, and bitwise operators.

Arithmetic Operators

The arithmetic operators include the four basic arithmetic operations, as well as the modulus operator (%) that is used to obtain the division remainder.

```
x = 3 + 2; // 5 - addition
x = 3 - 2; // 1 - subtraction
x = 3 * 2; // 6 - multiplication
x = 3 / 2; // 1.5 - division
x = 3 % 2; // 1 - modulus (division remainder)
```

Assignment Operators

The second group is the assignment operators. Most important, the assignment operator (=) itself, which assigns a value to a variable.

```
x = 0; // assignment
```

Combined Assignment Operators

A common use of the assignment and arithmetic operators is to operate on a variable and then to save the result back into that same variable. These operations can be shortened with the combined assignment operators.

```
x += 5; // x = x+5;
x -= 5; // x = x-5;
x *= 5; // x = x*5;
x /= 5; // x = x/5;
x %= 5; // x = x%5;
```

Increment and Decrement Operators

Another common operation is to increment or decrement a variable by one. This can be simplified with the increment (++) and decrement (--) operators.

```
x++; // x = x+1;
x--; // x = x-1;
```

Both of these can be used either before or after a variable.

```
x++; // post-increment
x--; // post-decrement
++x; // pre-increment
--x; // pre-decrement
```

The result on the variable is the same whichever is used. The difference is that the post-operator returns the original value before it changes the variable, while the pre-operator changes the variable first and then returns the value.

```
x = 5; y = x++; // y=5, x=6
x = 5; y = ++x; // y=6, x=6
```

Comparison Operators

The comparison operators compare two values and return either true or false. They are mainly used to specify conditions, which are expressions that evaluate to either true or false.

```
x = (2 == 3);  // false - equal to
x = (2 === 3); // false - identical
x = (2 !== 3); // true - not identical
x = (2 != 3);  // true - not equal to
x = (2 > 3);   // false - greater than
x = (2 < 3);   // true - less than
x = (2 >= 3);  // false - greater than or equal to
x = (2 <= 3);  // true - less than or equal to
```

The strict equality operators, === and !==, are used for comparing both type and value. These are necessary because the regular equal to (==) and not equal to (!=) operators will automatically perform a type conversion before they compare the operands.

```
x = (1 == "1");  // true (same value)
x = (1 === "1"); // false (different types)
```

It is considered good practice to use strict comparison when the type conversion feature of the equal to operation is not needed.

Logical Operators

The logical operators are often used together with the comparison operators. Logical and (&&) evaluates to true if both the left and right sides are true, and logical or (||) is true if either the left or right side is true. For inverting a Boolean result there is the logical not (!) operator. Note that for both "logical and" and "logical or," the right-hand side will not be evaluated if the result is already determined by the left-hand side.

```
x = (true && false); // false - logical and
x = (true || false); // true - logical or
x = !(true);         // false - logical not
```

Bitwise Operators

The bitwise operators can manipulate the individual bits that make up an integer. For example, the right shift operator (>>) moves all bits except the sign bit to the right, whereas zero-fill right shift (>>>) moves all bits right including the sign bit. Both of these operators evaluate the same for positive numbers.

```
x = 5 & 4;  // 101 & 100 = 100 (4) - and
x = 5 | 4;  // 101 | 100 = 101 (5) - or
x = 5 ^ 4;  // 101 ^ 100 = 001 (1) - xor
x = 4 << 1; // 100 << 1 =1000 (8) - left shift
x = 4 >> 1; // 100 >> 1 = 010 (2) - right shift
x = 4 >>>1; // 100 >>> 1 = 010 (2) - zero-fill right shift
x = ~4;     // ~00000100 = 11111011 (-5) - invert
```

The bitwise operators also have combined assignment operators.

```
x=5; x &= 4;  // 101 & 100 = 100 (4) - and
x=5; x |= 4;  // 101 | 100 = 101 (5) - or
x=5; x ^= 4;  // 101 ^ 100 = 001 (1) - xor
x=4; x <<= 1; // 100 << 1 =1000 (8) - left shift
x=4; x >>= 1; // 100 >> 1 = 010 (2) - right shift
x=4; x >>>=1; // 100 >>> 1 = 010 (2) - right shift
```

Keep in mind that JavaScript numbers are stored as double precision floating-point numbers. However, the bitwise operations need to operate on integers and therefore numbers are temporarily converted to 32-bit signed integers when bitwise operations are performed.

Operator Precedence

In JavaScript, expressions are normally evaluated from left to right. However, when an expression contains multiple operators, the precedence of those operators decides the order that they are evaluated in. The order of precedence can be seen in the following table, where the operator with the lowest precedence will be evaluated first. This same order also applies to many other languages, such as PHP and Java.

Pre	Operator	Pre	Operator
1	() [] . x++ x--	8	&
2	! ~ ++x --x	9	^
3	* / %	10	|
4	+ -	11	&&
5	<< >> >>>	12	||
6	< <= > >=	13	= op=
7	== != === !===	14	,

To give an example, multiplication binds harder than addition and will therefore be evaluated first in the following line of code.

```
x = 4 + 3 * 2; // 10
```

This can be clarified by enclosing the part of the expression that will be evaluated first in parentheses. As seen in the table, parentheses have the lowest precedence of all operators.

```
x = 4 + (3 * 2); // 10
```

CHAPTER 4

Arrays

An array is a data structure used for storing a collection of values. JavaScript arrays can be grouped into three kinds: numeric, associative, and multidimensional. The distinction between these arrays is only conceptual, as JavaScript considers them all to be array objects.

Numeric Arrays

Numeric arrays store each element in the array with a numeric index. An empty array can be created using the array constructor in the following way.

```
var a = new Array(); // empty array
```

To add elements to the array you can reference them one at a time by placing the element's index inside square brackets. Assigning a value to an element automatically creates space for that element and increases the capacity of the array. Note that the array index starts with zero.

```
a[0] = 1;
a[1] = 2;
a[2] = 3;
```

The initial capacity of an array can be specified by passing a single numeric parameter to the array constructor. This can be used to improve performance in cases where the number of elements that the array will hold is known in advance.

```
var b = new Array(3);
```

Passing more than one argument, or a non-numeric argument, to the array constructor will instead assign those values to the first elements of the array.

```
var c = new Array(1, 2, 3);
```

Another method for creating an array is to include the element values inside square brackets, a so-called array literal. This is the shortest and most commonly used way to create arrays.

```
var d = [1, 2, 3];
```

Leaving out the values from the array literal provides a shortcut for creating an empty array.

```
var e = []; // empty array
```

The content of an array is accessed by referencing the index of the desired element inside the square brackets.

```
var f = [1, 2, 3];
document.write(f[0] + f[1] + f[2]); // "6"
```

If the referenced element does not exist, an object of the undefined type is returned.

```
document.write(f[3]); // "undefined"
```

Note that just as regular variables the elements inside of an array can store any data type or combination thereof.

```
var mixed = [0, 3.14, "string", true];
```

Associative Arrays

The associative array uses a key string to identify an element instead of a numeric index. To create one, first declare an empty array and then assign values to the desired keys.

```
var g = new Array();
g["name"] = "Peter";
g["age"] = 25;
```

When accessing these elements it is important to remember the key names since these arrays cannot be accessed with an index.

```
document.write(g["name"] + " is " + g["age"]); // "Peter is 25"
```

Arrays in JavaScript are objects and their elements are object properties. Therefore, elements of associative arrays can alternatively be referenced using the dot notation.

```
var h = new Array();
h.name = "Peter";
h.age = 25;
document.write(h.name + " is " + h.age); // "Peter is 25"
```

14

Numeric elements cannot be accessed in this way and must be referenced using the bracket notation.

```
h[0] = 1;
```

It is possible to mix numeric and associative elements in the same array as JavaScript makes no distinction between them. In fact, indices are stored as key strings behind the scenes and may alternatively be referenced as such.

```
h["0"] = 1;
```

Multidimensional Arrays

Arrays can be made multidimensional by adding arrays as elements to another array.

```
var m = [ ["00","01"], ["10","11"] ];
```

Multidimensional arrays can have any number of dimensions, but more than two dimensions are rarely needed. For each extra dimension another set of square brackets is added.

```
document.write(m[1][1]); // "11"
```

Unlike many other languages, multidimensional arrays in JavaScript do not need to have the same length of all sub-arrays. The dimensions can also be changed later in the script as the array capacity is automatically adjusted.

```
m[1][2] = "12";
```

Array Object

The array object provides access to a number of members useful for manipulating arrays. One such member is the length property, which retrieves or sets the current capacity of the array.

```
var x = [1, 2, 3];
var len = x.length; // 3
x.length = 2; // deletes third element
document.write(x[2]); // "undefined"
```

Code hints in your IDE provide a list of the members available to the array object. To give an example, the pop method removes the last element from the array, and push appends one or more elements to the end of the array.

```
var y = [1, 2];
y.push(3); // add element to end of array

y.pop(); // remove last element
```

CHAPTER 5

Strings

A string consists of a series of characters delimited by either double quotes or single quotes. Which notation to use is a matter of preference.

```
var s1 = "Hello";
var s2 = ' World';
```

There are two operators that can operate on strings. For combining strings there is the plus sign (+), which is called the concatenation operator in this context. It has an accompanying assignment operator (+=) that appends a string to the end of a string variable.

```
var greeting = s1 + s2; // "Hello World"
s1 += s2; // "Hello World"
```

To break a line within a string, a backslash must be added. This character escapes the newline character that in JavaScript normally means the end of a statement. The backslash and line break are both removed from the value of the string.

```
greeting = "Hello \
World";
```

Escape Characters

Escape characters are used to write special characters, such as new lines and tabs. These characters are always preceded by a backslash "\". For instance, to insert a single-quote mark inside a single-quoted string the mark needs to be preceded with a backslash.

```
var s = 'It\'s'; // "It's"
```

The following table lists the escape characters available in JavaScript.

Character	Meaning	Character	Meaning
\n	newline	\f	form feed
\t	horizontal tab	\v	vertical tab
\'	single quote	\"	double quote
\b	backspace	\r	carriage return
\\	backslash		

In addition to these escape characters there are also notations for referencing the Unicode and Latin-1 encoded character sets. Unicode characters are expressed as "\u" followed by a 4-digit hexadecimal number. Latin-1 characters can be represented either as a three-digit octal number or a two-digit hexadecimal number starting with "\x". This is illustrated below where the new line character is represented in four different ways.

```
var line = '\n'; // escape code
    line = '\012'; // octal Latin-1
    line = '\x0A'; // hexadecimal Latin-1
    line = '\u000A'; // hexadecimal Unicode
```

Strings and Numbers

In an expression that involves both a string and a numeric value, the concatenation operator will convert the number to a string. Other numeric operators will attempt to convert the string to a number if possible, or else evaluate as NaN.

```
"5" + 5; // "55"
"5" - 5; // 0
"a" - 5; // NaN
```

A numeric value that is represented as a string can be converted to a whole number using the parseInt function.

```
parseInt("5") + 5; // 10
```

Similarly, parseFloat can be used to convert a string to a floating-point number. For both these functions only the first number in the string is returned, or else the method returns NaN if the first character is not a number.

```
parseFloat("3.14"); // 3.14
parseFloat("Hi"); // NaN
```

Alternatively, the unary addition operator (+) may be used to perform the string to numeric conversion, by placing the addition sign just before the string.

```
+"5" + 5; // 10
```

String Object

All strings in JavaScript are string objects. As such they provide quick access to properties and methods that are useful when performing common string operations. For example, the number of characters in a string can be determined using the length property.

```
var a = "Hello";
var len = a.length; // 5
```

Your IDE provides code hints as you type the dot to access the members of a string object, giving you a full list of the available members. For instance, the toLowerCase method converts the string to lowercase letters. The resulting string is returned without changing the original string.

```
var lower = a.toLowerCase(); // "hello"
```

JavaScript interprets any piece of text as an instance of the string object. Therefore, it is possible to call methods directly on string constants just as it can be done on string variables.

```
var upper = "abc".toUpperCase(); // "ABC";
```

CHAPTER 6

Conditionals

Conditional statements are used to execute different code blocks based on different conditions.

If Statement

The if statement only executes if the expression inside the parentheses is evaluated to true. In JavaScript, this does not have to be a Boolean expression. It can be any expression, in which case zero, null, NaN, empty strings, and undefined variables are evaluated as false, and all other values are true.

```
if (x < 1) {
  document.write("x < 1");
}
```

To test for other conditions, the if statement can be extended by any number of else if clauses. Each additional condition will only be tested if the preceding conditions are false.

```
else if (x > 1) {
  document.write("x > 1");
}
```

For handling all other cases there can be one else clause at the end, which will execute if all previous conditions are false.

```
else {
  document.write("x == 1");
}
```

The curly brackets can be left out if only a single statement needs to be executed conditionally. However, it is considered good practice to always include them since they improve code readability.

```
if (x < 1)
  document.write("x < 1");
else if (x > 1)
  document.write("x > 1");
else
  document.write("x == 1");
```

Switch Statement

The switch statement checks for equality between an expression and a series of case labels, and then passes execution to the matching case. The expression can be of any type and will be matched against the case labels using strict comparison (===). Switches may contain any number of case clauses, and it can end with a default label for handling all other cases.

```
switch (x) {
  case 0: document.write("x is 0"); break;
  case 1: document.write("x is 1"); break;
  default: document.write("x is not 0 or 1"); break;
}
```

Note that the statements after each case label end with the break keyword to skip the rest of the switch. If the break is left out, execution will fall through to the next case, which can be useful if several cases need to be evaluated in the same way.

Ternary Operator

In addition to the if and switch statements there is the ternary operator (?:), which provides a shortcut for a single if else statement. This operator takes three expressions. If the first one is true, then the second expression is evaluated and returned; and if it is false, the third one is evaluated and returned.

```
// Ternary operator expression
y = (x === 1) ? 1 : 2;
```

In JavaScript, this operator can also be used as a stand-alone code statement, and not just as an expression.

```
// Ternary operator statement
(x === 1) ? y = 1 : y = 2;
```

The programming term expression refers to code that evaluates to a value, whereas a statement is a code segment that ends with a semicolon or a closing curly bracket.

CHAPTER 7

Loops

The loop statements are used to execute a code block several times. JavaScript has four kinds of loops: while, do-while, for, and for-in. As with the conditional if statement, the curly brackets for these loops can be omitted if there is only one statement in the code block.

While Loop

The while loop runs through the code block only if its condition is true, and will continue looping for as long as the condition remains true.

```
var i = 0;
while (i < 10) {
  document.write(i++); // 0-9
}
```

The loop here will print out the numbers 0 to 9. Bear in mind that the condition is only checked at the start of each iteration.

Do-While Loop

The do-while loop works in the same way as the while loop, except that it checks the condition after the code block. It will therefore always run through the code block at least once. Note that this loop ends with a semicolon.

```
var j = 0;
do {
  document.write(j++); // 0-9
} while (j < 10);
```

For Loop

The for loop runs through a code block a specific number of times. It uses three parameters. The first one initializes a counter and is always executed once before the loop. The second parameter holds the condition for the loop and is checked before each iteration. The third parameter contains the increment of the counter and is executed at the end of each iteration.

```
for (var k = 0; k < 10; k++) {
  document.write(k); // 0-9
}
```

This loop has several variations since either one of the parameters can be left out. For example, if the first and third parameters are left out, it behaves in the same way as the while loop.

```
var k;
for (; k < 10;) {
  document.write(k++); // 0-9
}
```

The first and third parameters can also be split into several statements using the comma operator (,).

```
for (var k = 0, m = 0; k < 10; k++, m--) {
  document.write(k+m); // 000... (10x)
}
```

The length property retrieves the number of elements in an array. Together with the for loop it can be used to iterate through an array.

```
var a = [1, 2, 3];
for (var i = 0; i < a.length; i++) {
  document.write(a[i]); // "123"
}
```

If there is no need to keep track of iterations the for-in loop provides a shorter syntax for traversing arrays.

For-in Loop

The for-in loop provides an easy way of iterating through elements in an array or through properties in an object. On each iteration the key or index of the next property is assigned to the variable, and the loop continues to iterate until it has gone through all members of the object.

```
var colors = ["red","green","blue"];
for (i in colors) {
  document.write(colors[i] + " "); // "red green blue"
}
```

Break and Continue

There are two jump statements that can be used inside loops: break and continue. The break keyword ends the loop structure and continue skips the rest of the current iteration and continues at the beginning of the next iteration.

```
for (var i = 0; i < 10; i++)
{
  if (i == 2) continue;    // start next iteration
  else if (i == 5) break; // end loop
  document.write(i);       // "0134"
}
```

To break out of a loop above the current one, the outer loop must first be labeled by adding a name followed by a colon before that outer loop. With this label in place it can now be used as an argument to the break statement, telling it which loop to break out of. This also works with the continue keyword, in order to skip to the next iteration of the named loop.

```
myloop:
for (var i = 0; i < 10; i++)
{
  var j = 0;
  while (++j < 10)
  {
    break myloop; // end for loop
  }
}
```

CHAPTER 8

Functions

Functions are reusable code blocks that will only execute when called. They allow developers to divide their scripts into smaller parts that are easier to understand and reuse.

Defining Functions

To create a function the function keyword is used followed by a name, a set of parentheses, and a code block. The naming convention for functions is the same as for variables – to use a descriptive name with each word initially capitalized, except for the first one.

```
function myFunc()
{
  document.write("Hello World");
}
```

This function simply displays a text string to the web document. A function code block can contain any JavaScript code, including other function definitions.

Calling Functions

Once defined a function can be called (invoked) from anywhere on the document, by typing its name followed by a set of parentheses. Function names are case sensitive, so the capitalization of letters needs to be consistent.

```
myFunc(); // "Hello World"
```

A function can be called even if the function definition appears later in the script. This is because declarations in JavaScript are processed before code is executed.

```
foo(); // ok
function foo() {}
```

Function Parameters

The parentheses that follow the function's name are used for passing arguments to the function. To do this the corresponding parameters must first be added to the function's parameter list. These parameters can then be used in the function as regular variables.

```
function sum(a, b) {
  var sum = a + b;
  console.log(sum);
}
```

A function can be defined to take any number of arguments. When the function is called the arguments are provided in the form of a comma-separated list. In this example, the function accepts two numeric arguments and displays their sum.

```
sum(2, 3); // "5"
```

Like variables, function parameters do not have types specified in their declarations. Therefore no type checking is automatically performed, and function arguments are not limited to any specific data type.

Variable Parameter Lists

It is permitted to call a function with a different number of arguments than it has been defined to accept. If a function is called with fewer arguments, then the remaining parameters will be set to undefined.

```
function say(message) {
  console.log(message);
}
say(); // "undefined"
```

When a function is called with more parameters than in its definition, the extra parameters will be nameless. It is possible to reference these extra parameters through the array-like arguments object, which contains all parameters passed to the function.

```
function say() {
  console.log(arguments[0]);
}
say("Hello"); // "Hello"
```

The arguments object can be used to create varadic functions, which are functions able to handle different numbers of arguments. To give an example, any number of arguments can be passed to the following function. The function iterates through the arguments and combines them into a string that it prints to the console.

```
function combine() {
   var result = "";
   for (var i = 0; i < arguments.length; i++) {
      result += arguments[i];
   }
   console.log(result);
}
combine(1, 2, 3); // "123";
```

Return Statement

Return is a jump statement that causes the function to exit and return the specified value to the place where the function was called. To illustrate, the following function returns the sum of its two arguments. This function can, in turn, be passed as an argument to another function, where it will evaluate to the resulting number.

```
function getSum(a, b) {
   return a + b; // exit function and return value
}
console.log( getSum(1, 2) ); // "3"
```

The return statement can also be used as a way to exit a function before the end block is reached without returning any specific value. Functions without a return value will implicitly return undefined.

```
function foo() {
   return; // exit function
}
console.log( foo() ); // "undefined"
```

Just like variables and parameters, return values are not type checked. Functions need to be properly documented for users of the functions to know what their inputs and outputs are supposed to be.

Argument Passing

Arguments are passed to functions by value. For primitive types this means that only a copy of the value is passed to the function. Therefore, changing the parameter in any way will not affect the original variable.

```
function set(y) {
   y = 1;
}
var x = 0;
set(x); // copy of value passed
console.log(x); // "0"
```

When an object type is used as an argument it is the reference to that object that is passed. This allows the function to make changes to the original object's properties.

```
function addFruit(basket) {
  basket[0] = "Apple";
}
var fruits = [];
addFruit(fruits); // copy of reference passed
console.log( fruits[0] ); // "Apple"
```

Assigning a new object to the parameter will not affect the original object outside the function. This is because the assignment changes the value of the parameter rather than the value of one of the object's properties.

```
function makeFruit(basket) {
  basket = [ "Apple" ];
}
var fruits = [];
makeFruit(fruits);
console.log( fruits[0] ); // "undefined"
```

Function Expressions

Functions in JavaScript are objects, specifically function objects. As such they can be assigned to variables and passed to other functions just like any other object. When a function is used in this way it is called a function expression, as opposed to a function declaration. A function expression can be assigned to a variable using the normal assignment syntax, including the semicolon.

```
var say = function foo(message)
{
  console.log("Hello " + message);
};
```

When calling a function object the name of the variable is referenced instead of the function's name.

```
say("World"); // "Hello World"
```

The function name can be used inside the function to refer to itself, but the name is otherwise unnecessary. As such the name is typically omitted. The function expression then becomes known as an anonymous function.

```
var say = function(message)
{
  console.log("Hello " + message);
};
```

Functional expressions are usually used as callback functions that are either passed into or returned from other functions. They allow code to be written very concisely since the function can be inlined without having to define it somewhere else. To illustrate, the following example uses the window.setTimeout function, which takes another function along with a number as its arguments. The number specifies how many milliseconds it will wait before the function argument is called.

```
// Call anonymous function after one second
window.setTimeout(function() { console.log("Hello") }, 1000);
```

Scope and Lifetime

The scope of a variable refers to the region of code within which it is possible to use that variable. Variables in JavaScript may be declared either globally or locally. A global variable is declared outside of any functions and is accessible from anywhere in the document. A local variable, on the other hand, is declared inside of a function and will only be accessible within that function.

```
var globalVar = 0; // global variable

function foo() {
  var localVar = 0; // local variable
}
```

The lifetime of a local variable is limited. Whereas a global variable will remain allocated for the duration of the script, a local variable will be destroyed when its function has finished executing.

```
console.log(globalVar); // "0"
foo();
console.log(localVar); // throws a ReferenceError
```

When two variables in scope have the same name, there is a name conflict. More inner scopes take precedence, so the innermost scope takes the highest precedence, while the outermost scope takes the lowest.

```
var a = "global";

function foo() {
  var a = "local"; // overshaddows global variable
  console.log(a);
}
```

```
foo(); // "local"
console.log(a); // "global"
```

In contrast to many other languages, code blocks in JavaScript do not have their own scope. A variable defined in a control structure code block – such as a loop or conditional statement – will therefore not be destroyed when the block ends.

```
if(true) {
  var x = 10; // global variable
}

console.log(x); // "10"
```

There is an alternative way of creating variables by assigning a value to an undeclared variable without the use of the var keyword. This will implicitly declare the variable as a global variable, even if it is declared within a function.

```
function foo() {
  a = 5; // global variable
}
foo();
console.log(a); // "5"
```

Mistakenly introducing or overriding global variables in this way is a common source of bugs. It is therefore recommended to always explicitly declare variables with the var keyword.

```
var a = 10;
foo(); // replaces value of global variable
console.log(a); // "5"
```

Like function declarations, explicit variable declarations are also processed before the script is executed. Variables can therefore be referenced in the code before they are declared.

```
console.log(a); // "undefined"
var a = "defined";
console.log(a); // "defined"
```

This behavior is different for implicitly declared variables, because such variables do not exist until the code assigning them a value is run.

```
console.log(b); // throws a ReferenceError

b = "defined"; // never executes
```

CHAPTER 9

Objects

An object is a collection of named values known as properties. Properties can be either variables that hold the state of the object, or functions that define what the object can do. The appeal of objects is that they provide functionality while hiding their inner workings. All you need to know is what an object can do for you, not how it does it.

Object Properties

An empty object can be created using the new directive in the following explicit manner.

```
var box = new Object();
```

Properties for an object are created automatically when they are assigned to, using either the dot notation or the array notation.

```
box.x = 2;
box["y"] = 3;
```

Likewise, properties can be referenced in one of these two ways.

```
console.log(box.x);      // "2"
console.log(box["y"]); // "3"
```

A property can be removed from its object with the delete directive. This cannot be done with regular variables, only with object properties.

```
box.z = 1;    // add property
delete box.z; // delete property
```

To check if an object contains a property, the in operator can be used. The property name is then specified as a string.

```
console.log("x" in box); // "true"
console.log("z" in box); // "false"
```

Object Methods

A function can be added to an object in the form of a property. Such a function is referred to as a method. When referencing a function declaration the parentheses are left out.

```
box.getArea = myArea;
function myArea() { return this.x * this.y; }
```

The this keyword used here is a reference to the object that currently owns the function. In case the function is called outside an object context, the keyword will instead refer to the window object. To prevent such out-of-context calls, it is better to inline the function using a function expression. This also prevents the function's name from unnecessarily cluttering up the global namespace.

```
box.getArea = function() { return this.x * this.y; };
```

Once bound to the object the method can be invoked in the familiar way. The this keyword will here refer to the box object, which had the properties x and y defined earlier.

```
console.log( box.getArea() ); // "6"
```

Object Literals

A shorter way to create an object is to use an object literal, which is delimited by a set of curly brackets. When creating an empty object the brackets are empty.

```
var box = {};
```

The advantage of using an object literal is that the properties can be set when the object is created, by including them within the curly brackets. Each name-value pair of a property is separated by a colon, and each property in turn is separated by a comma.

```
var box = {
  x: 2,
  y: 3,
  getArea: function() { return this.x * this.y; }
};
```

Object literals are useful if only a single instance of an object is needed. If more than one instance is required a function constructor can be used instead.

Constructor Functions

Objects can be created from a constructor function. They provide features that classes provide in other languages, by allowing multiple instances of an object to be created from a single set of definitions. By convention, functions intended to be used as object constructors start with a capital letter, as a reminder of their purpose.

```
function Box(x, y) {
  this.x = x;
  this.y = y;
  this.getArea = function() { return this.x * this.y; };
}
```

To instantiate one or more objects from this constructor the function is called with the new directive. Just like any other function, a constructor can accept arguments, as seen in this example.

```
var b1 = new Box(1, 2);
var b2 = new Box(3, 4);
```

Each object instance contains its own set of properties, which can hold values that are different from those of other instances.

```
console.log(b1.x); // "1"
console.log(b2.x); // "3"
```

The constructor function previously defined includes a function declared within another function. Such a nested function can access variables defined in its parent function, as it forms a so-called closure that includes the scope of the outer function. An advantage of this object creation pattern is that it provides information hiding. For instance, the following example has a method that uses a local variable to record how many times the method has been called. This feature is similar to private properties in class-based languages, as the local variable is only visible from within the constructor function.

```
function Counter(x, y) {
  var count = 0;
  this.printCount = function() { console.log(count++); };
}
```

```
var c = new Counter();
c.printCount(); // "0";
c.printCount(); // "1";
```

A small disadvantage of this object creation pattern is that each instance will have its own printCount method, which increases the memory consumed by each object. An alternative pattern that avoids this is to make use of inheritance to add the method to the object's prototype instead.

Inheritance

An object can inherit properties from another object. This provides a way for objects to reuse code from other objects. The specialized object is commonly called the child, and the more general object is called the parent.

In JavaScript, inheritance is achieved through a prototypical inheritance model. In this model each object has an internal property that acts as a link to another object, called its prototype. Consider the following object.

```
var myObj = new Object();
```

This object inherits properties from the built-in Object constructor. When a property is requested that the object does not directly contain, JavaScript will automatically search up the inheritance chain until either the requested property is found or the end of the chain is reached.

```
// Add a property to myObj
myObj.x = 5;
// Call a method from Object
myObj.hasOwnProperty("x"); // true
```

The last link in the chain is always the built-in Object constructor, whose prototype link in turn is null, which marks the end of the chain. A reference to the object's prototype link can be retrieved using the __proto__ property. This is not to be confused with the prototype property of the constructor function, which is the literal object representation of the function that gets assigned to __proto__ when a new instance of that function is created.

```
myObj.__proto__ === Object.prototype; // true
myObj.__proto__.__proto__ === null;   // true
```

Inheritance is achieved by expanding the prototype chain. This can be done in the constructor function, by setting the prototype property to the object that is to be inherited.

```
function Parent() { this.a = "Parent"; }
function Child() { }
Child.prototype = new Parent();
var child = new Child();
console.log(child.a); // "Parent"
```

Type Checking

You can manually confirm the type of an object by comparing its __proto__ link to the prototype property of a constructor function.

```
child.__proto__ === Child.prototype; // true
```

JavaScript also provides the `instanceof` operator. This operator navigates through the prototype chain and returns true if the left-side object points to the right-side constructor anywhere in the prototype chain.

```
child instanceof Child;  // true
child instanceof Parent; // true
child instanceof Object; // true
```

Object Create

Another way to perform inheritance is through the `Object.create` method. This method provides a simpler way to implement inheritance, by allowing an object to directly inherit from another object without the use of an additional construction function.

```
var p = new Parent();
var c1 = Object.create(p); // inherit from p
```

An optional second argument to the method allows you to initialize properties for the object using a special notation.

```
var c2 = Object.create(p, { name: { value: "Child 2" } } );
console.log(c2.name); // "Child 2"
```

The prototype property of an object can be used to dynamically add properties to the prototype. This causes all objects linking to that prototype to inherit the new properties.

```
Parent.prototype.x = "new property";
console.log(c2.x); // "new property"
```

As shown in this chapter, JavaScript offers a lot of flexibility when it comes to creating and using objects. The choice of which method to use often comes down to a matter of preference.

CHAPTER 10

■ ■ ■

Document Object Model

The Document Object Model or DOM is a programming interface that describes all elements of a web document and how they are related to each other. It is through this interface that JavaScript code can interact with the web document.

DOM Nodes

In the DOM model, the content of the web document is represented in a tree-like structure consisting of nodes. By knowing how these nodes are organized, it becomes possible to change any part of the document dynamically. Consider the following HTML markup.

```
<p>My paragraph</p>
```

This markup creates two nodes in the DOM tree: an element node and a text node. Element nodes can have children, and the text node here is a child of the paragraph element. Conversely, the paragraph node is the parent of the text node. Moving on to the next example, there are four nodes.

```
<div id="mydiv">
  <!-- My comment -->
</div>
```

The div element node contains three nodes: two text nodes and one comment node. The extra text nodes come from the whitespace (spaces, tabs, and newlines) found before and after the comment in this example. All four of these nodes are invisible when viewing the web page.

Each element can have an optional id attribute, as applied to the div element in this example. Because this attribute must be unique, it provides a convenient way of selecting a specific node in the DOM tree. Note that attributes are also considered to be nodes by the DOM specification; however, when it comes to navigating the DOM tree, the attribute nodes are instead viewed as properties of element nodes.

Selecting Nodes

The document object represents the web document and provides several ways to access the DOM tree and retrieve node references. The most common way is to use the getElementById method. This method returns a reference to the element with the specified unique id. Using this method the div element node from the previous example can be retrieved.

```
var mydiv = document.getElementById("mydiv");
```

Elements can also be selected by their tag name with the getElementsByTagName method. This method retrieves an array-like collection of all elements of that type.

```
var mydivs = document.getElementsByTagName("div");
```

Another less common way of selecting elements is through the class attribute. As multiple elements can share the same class name, this method also returns a collection. It is supported in all modern browsers excluding IE<9.

```
var myclasses = document.getElementsByClassName("myclass");
```

The getElementById method can only be invoked from the document object, but the other two methods may alternatively be called from a specific node in the DOM tree to only search the children of that node. For instance, the following code retrieves all element nodes beneath the body element.

```
var myelements = document.body.getElementsByTagName("*");
```

In addition to the body node, the document object also has properties for retrieving references to the html and head nodes.

```
var htmlnode = document.documentElement;
var headnode = document.head;
var bodynode = document.body;
```

Element nodes can also be located using the querySelector method. This method returns the first element that matches the specified CSS selector, which in this case is the first element with its class attribute set to myclass.

```
var mynode = document.querySelector(".myclass");
```

Similarly, the querySelectorAll method retrieves a collection of all element nodes that match the given CSS query. Both of these query methods are supported by all modern browsers, excluding IE<9.

```
var mynodes = document.querySelectorAll(".myclass");
```

If no elements are found, null is returned. This behavior is consistent across all DOM methods.

Traversing DOM Tree

Once a node is selected, there are a number of properties that allows the DOM tree to be traversed relative to that node. The following list can be used to illustrate.

```
<ul id="mylist">
  <li>First</li>
  <li>Second</li>
  <li>Third</li>
</ul>
```

A reference to this unordered list node is here retrieved by its id.

```
var mylist = document.getElementById("mylist");
```

Element nodes below this node are available through the children collection. The first list item can also be retrieved using the firstElementChild property.

```
var first = mylist.children[0];
first = mylist.firstElementChild;
```

Likewise, the last node can be accessed through either the children collection or the lastElementChild property.

```
var third = mylist.children[2];
third = mylist.lastElementChild;
```

The DOM tree can be navigated left and right to neighboring nodes using the previousElementSibling and nextElementSibling properties. Siblings in this case refers to nodes that share the same parent.

```
var second = first.nextElementSibling;
second = third.previousElementSibling;
```

These four properties – firstElementChild, lastElementChild, nextElementSibling, and previousElementSibling – are supported by all modern browsers, except IE<9. For full browser support, the following properties can be used instead: firstChild, lastChild, nextSibling, and previousSibling. Bear in mind that these properties also take text and comment nodes into account, not just element nodes.

The parentNode property references the parent node. Together with the other properties, they allow the DOM tree to be traversed in all four directions: up, down, left, and right.

```
mylist = first.parentNode;
```

The children collection contains only element nodes. An exception to this is in IE versions prior to 9, where this collection also includes comment nodes. If all node types are needed, the childNodes collection is used instead. This collection contains all node children, including element, text, and comment nodes. Once more IE<9 behaves differently from other browsers, by not including whitespace-only text nodes in the childNodes collection.

```
mylist.childNodes[0]; // whitespace text node
mylist.childNodes[1]; // li node
mylist.childNodes[2]; // whitespace text node
```

For element nodes both the nodeName and tagName properties contain the name of the tag in uppercase letters. They can be used to test the tag name of an element node.

```
if (mydiv.nodeName == "DIV")
  console.log(mydiv.tagName); // "DIV"
```

While the tagName property is meant specifically for element nodes, the nodeName property is useful for any node type. For instance, comment nodes evaluate to "#comment" and text nodes to "#text".

```
mylist.childNodes[0].nodeName; // #text
mylist.childNodes[1].nodeName; // LI
mylist.childNodes[2].nodeName; // #text
```

Creating Nodes

Nodes in the DOM can be dynamically added, removed, or changed. To illustrate, a new list item will be added to the previous list. The first step is to create the element and text nodes, using the createElement and createTextNode methods respectively.

```
var myitem = document.createElement('li');
var mytext = document.createTextNode("New list item");
```

The text node is then added to the element node, using the appendChild method on the list item node.

```
myitem.appendChild(mytext);
```

Next, the list item node is added to the unordered list using the same method. This causes the new list item to appear on the page.

```
mylist.appendChild(myitem);
```

The appendChild method adds its node argument as the last child of the element node it is called from. To insert the node somewhere else, the insertBefore method is used. This method takes a second node argument, before which the new node is inserted.

```
mylist.insertBefore(myitem, mylist.children[0]);
```

A node cannot be in two places at the same time, so this action removes the node previously added to the end of the list and instead places it in the beginning. To add another similar node the element can first be copied using the cloneNode method. This method takes a Boolean argument, which specifies whether the element's descendant nodes will also be copied.

```
var newitem = myitem.cloneNode(false);
```

This node is next added to the end of the list, but because it was cloned without its descendants it has no text node and so it appears as an empty list element in the document.

```
mylist.appendChild(newitem);
```

As shown before, the text node can be created and linked using the createTextNode and appendChild methods. A shorter alternative is to instead modify the innerHTML property, which represents the HTML content of the element.

```
newitem.innerHTML = "<b>Another</b> new list item";
```

This property allows for both element and text nodes to be created automatically. Another similar property that is useful to know of is textContent. This property represents the content of the element stripped of any HTML tags.

```
newitem.textContent; // "Another new list item"
newitem.innerHTML;   // "<b>Another</b> new list item"
```

Removing Nodes

A node can be removed using the removeChild method. This method returns a reference to the removed node: in this case, the last child in the list. Keep in mind that catching return values in JavaScript is optional.

```
var removedNode = mylist.removeChild(mylist.lastElementChild);
```

Another way to remove a node is to replace it with a different node. This is done with the replaceChild method, which also returns the replaced node. The following code replaces the first child of the list with the previously removed node.

```
mylist.replaceChild(removedNode, mylist.firstElementChild);
```

Attribute Nodes

Attribute nodes are accessible through their containing element, as opposed to being child nodes of that element. To illustrate, here is a paragraph with an id attribute for easy selection.

```
<p id="myid">My paragraph</p>
```

Its element node is selected in the familiar way.

```
var mypara = document.getElementById("myid");
```

The setAttribute method adds an attribute to the referenced element, or replaces its value if it already exists. It takes two arguments: the attribute and the value.

```
mypara.setAttribute("class","myclass");
```

To retrieve the value for an attribute, the getAttribute method is used. Before the attribute is retrieved a check to make sure it exists is here performed using the hasAttribute method.

```
if (mypara.hasAttribute("class"))
  console.log(mypara.getAttribute("class")); // "myclass"
```

Attributes are automatically synchronized with properties of the element node. This provides a less verbose way to set and get attributes. Properties and their corresponding attributes share the same name, except for the class attribute whose property is called className. This is because class is a reserved keyword in JavaScript.

```
console.log(mypara.id);        // "myid"
console.log(mypara.className); // "myclass"
```

CSS properties for an element can be changed dynamically using the style attribute. One way to do so is to modify the attribute directly. This will overwrite any inline styles previously set through this attribute.

```
mypara.setAttribute("style", "background-color: yellow;");
```

To instead add a new style to the element, properties of the style object can be changed. These properties have the same name as their corresponding CSS property, except that any hyphens are removed and each word after the first one is capitalized.

```
mypara.style.backgroundColor = "yellow";
```

To revert a style change you just need to clear that property by setting it to an empty string.

```
mypara.style.backgroundColor = "";
```

CHAPTER 11

Events

Events are occurrences that take place in the interaction between the user, the web page, and the browser. Event handling enables a script to detect and react to these occurrences, allowing the web page to become interactive.

Event Handling

There are three steps to handling an event. First, you need to locate the element that will receive the event. Events always take place in the context of element nodes inside the DOM tree. In this example the event will occur when the following hyperlink is clicked.

```
<a href="http://www.google.com" id="mylink">My link</a>
```

The next step is to create an event handler, which is the code that will execute when the event occurs. This event handler typically consists of a function, which in this case displays an alert box with a message for the user.

```
function myEventHandler() {
  alert("Event triggered");
}
```

Finally, the last step is to register the event handler for the particular event that is to be handled. Here the link element node is selected, and the event handler is registered to its onclick event in the following way.

```
var mylink = document.getElementById("mylink");
mylink.onclick = myEventHandler;
```

When the user clicks on this link, the event handler is called and the alert box pops up. Once the box is closed, the default event handler takes over and the link is followed through as normal. To remove the event handler, the property is set to null.

```
mylink.onclick = null;
```

This is called the traditional model for event registration. Another, shorter registration method is the inline model, which uses event attributes to attach the event handler directly to the HTML element that produces the event.

```
<a href=" http://www.google.com" onclick="myEventHandler()">My link</a>
```

Note that the parentheses for the event handler are included in the inline model but not the traditional one. An even less verbose way of using this model is to also inline the function.

```
<a href=" http://www.google.com" onclick="alert('Event triggered')">My link</a>
```

An inlined event handler can contain more than one statement. In the following example, a return false statement is added to the event handler. This prevents the default browser action from taking place, which in this case means that the link will no longer be followed.

```
<a href=" http://www.google.com" onclick="alert('Event triggered'); return
false">My link</a>
```

Both the traditional and inline models are supported by all modern browsers. The traditional model is generally preferable, as it allows event handlers to be added, changed, and removed through code, and it completely separates the JavaScript from the HTML.

W3C standardized a third model for registering events in the DOM level 2 specification. In this W3C model, an event handler is added using the addEventListener method. This method takes three arguments: the event type, the event handler, and a Boolean value that will be looked at later.

```
mylink.addEventListener("click", myEventHandler, false);
```

Note that in the W3C model the "on" prefix of the event is left out, so "onclick" becomes just "click." To remove an event handler the removeEventListener is used with the same three arguments.

```
mylink.removeEventListener("click", myEventHandler, false);
```

The main advantage of the W3C model is that more than one event handler can be registered to the same event and for the same element node. A disadvantage is that it is not supported in IE<9, making it less cross-browser compatible than the other two methods.

Event Object

When an event is triggered, the browser passes an argument to the event handler representing the event as an object. This object can be accessed by adding a parameter to the event handler.

```
function myEventHandler(e) { }
```

This object is the W3C method for accessing event information. IE<9 passes no event object argument and instead has a global window.event object, which represents the last triggered event. For cross-browser compatibility, the following line can be added to the beginning of the handler to make sure the correct event object is retrieved in all browsers.

```
function myEventHandler(e) {
  if (!e) var e = window.event;
}
```

The event object provides additional information about the event through its properties. Different events have different properties, but all event objects have the type property. This property holds a string identifying the event, such as "click" for the onclick event.

```
console.log(e.type); // "click"
```

Most events also have a target, which is a reference to the element node that triggered the event. In the previous example this refers to the anchor element.

```
console.log(e.target.tagName); // "A"
```

On IE<9, the event object has a srcElement property instead of the target property. The cross-browser compatible way of retrieving the target is seen here.

```
var target = e.target || e.srcElement;
```

Event Propagation

Most DOM events have event propagation, meaning that an event triggered on an inner element will also trigger for outer elements. To illustrate, here is a paragraph element nested inside a div element.

```
<div id="outer">Outer element
  <p id="inner">Inner element</div>
</div>
```

The following code registers click events for both of these elements using the traditional model.

```
var inner = document.getElementById("inner");
inner.onclick = function() { alert("Inner"); }
var outer = document.getElementById("outer");
outer.onclick = function() { alert("Outer"); }
```

After an event triggers on the inner element, it then continues to trigger any event handlers attached to parents in nesting order. Therefore, clicking on the inner element will here display the "Inner" message first, followed by the "Outer" message. This default event order is called bubbling.

The reverse event order is called capturing. IE<9 has only the bubbling order, but all other modern browsers process event handlers first by capturing and then by bubbling. To register an event handler for the capturing phase, the last argument of addEventListener is set to true. In the following example, the numbers will be printed in order when the paragraph element is clicked.

```
outer.addEventListener("click", function() { console.log("1"); }, true);
inner.addEventListener("click", function() { console.log("2"); }, true);
inner.addEventListener("click", function() { console.log("3"); }, false);
outer.addEventListener("click", function() { console.log("4"); }, false);
```

When an event handler is triggered, it has the opportunity to prevent further event propagation by calling the stopPropagation method on the event object. In IE<9, the event's cancelBubble property needs to be set to true instead. The following is a cross-browser compatible way of stopping an event from propagating.

```
function cancelEvent(e) {
  if (!e) var e = window.event;
  e.cancelBubble = true;
  if (e.stopPropagation) e.stopPropagation();
}
```

DOM Events

There are many DOM events supported by modern browsers. Here is a list of the most common events you are likely to deal with.

Event Name	Description
onClick	Triggers when the user clicks an element. Can be applied to any visible element.
onLoad	Triggers on the window when the page has finished loading. Elements requiring external objects, such as <img>, <link>, and <iframe>, also have this event.
onMouseOver	Triggers when the user moves the mouse pointer onto an element.
onMouseOut	Triggers when the user moves the mouse pointer out of an element.
onSubmit	Triggers on <form> element when a form is submitted.
onFocus	Triggers when an element gains input focus. Most often used with form elements.
onBlur	Triggers when input focus is lost. Most often used with form elements.

The onload event is useful for initialization actions that require the whole document to be loaded. Remember that script blocks are run immediately when they appear in the document. They are therefore unable to directly change elements that appear later in the document, as illustrated in the following example.

```
<script>document.getElementById("para").style.color = "red";</script>
<p id="para">My paragraph</p>
```

The onload event provides a way to solve this by moving the initialization code to an event handler registered to that event. With this code in place the paragraph text is colored red once the document is loaded.

```
function colorText() {
  document.getElementById("para").style.color = "red";
}
window.addEventListener("load", colorText, false);
```

Notice that the onload event is registered for the window object, which represents the browser window. This is the top-most object in the DOM hierarchy to which the document object belongs, as well as all global code and variables.

To give another example, the onMouseOver and onMouseOut events are commonly used to create image rollover effects. The following sample code illustrates this by switching the displayed image when the user moves the mouse pointer over it.

```
<img src="pic1.png" id="rollover"
onmouseover = "document.getElementById('rollover').src='pic2.png'"
onmouseout = "document.getElementById('rollover').src='pic1.png'">
```

CHAPTER 12

Cookies

A cookie is a piece of data sent from a web site and stored locally on the user's computer. They provide a persistent storage space, allowing web sites to remember users as they move between pages or return to the site.

Creating Cookies

Cookies are created by assigning a name-value pair to the document.cookie object. They are limited to storing string values only.

```
document.cookie = "cookie1=mycookie";
```

The same object is used for retrieving the cookie string.

```
console.log(document.cookie); // "cookie1=mycookie"
```

To modify a cookie, you just need to assign it a new value. This will overwrite the previous cookie.

```
document.cookie = "cookie1=first";
```

When another name-value pair is assigned to the cookie object, another cookie is automatically created.

```
document.cookie = "cookie2=second";
```

Referencing the cookie object retrieves a string containing a semicolon-separated list of all cookies.

```
console.log("document.cookie"); // "cookie1=first;cookie2=second"
```

Each name-value pair can be extracted from the cookie string by using the split method of the string object. The method returns an array containing the split values, which are split according to the separator character specified as the argument.

```
var dataList = document.cookie.split(";");
console.log(dataList[0]); // "cookie1=first"
console.log(dataList[1]); // "cookie2=second"
```

Using split once more can separate the name from the value.

```
var pair = dataList[0].split("=");
console.log(pair[0] + " is " + pair[1]); // "cookie1 is first"
```

Encoding

The name-value pair of a cookie may not contain whitespace, commas, or semicolons. To ensure these characters are not included, the global escape method can be used to URL encode the string.

```
document.cookie = "cookie1=" + escape("Foo Bar");
```

In URL encoded form the space is replaced with %20.

```
console.log(document.cookie); // "cookie1=Foo%20Bar"
```

When reading the cookie string back the unescape method is used to undo the encoding.

```
console.log(unescape(document.cookie)); // "cookie1=Foo Bar"
```

Expiration Date

In addition to the name-value pair a cookie string can contain other information, such as when the cookie should expire. By default, the life span of a cookie is limited to the current browser session. This session ends when the user closes the window, after which the browser deletes the cookie. An expiration date is set in the following way, using the built-in Date object and its toGMTString method. This cookie is set to expire after one hour, by adding this number of milliseconds to the value returned by the getTime method.

```
var mycookie = "cookie1=first";
var date = new Date();
date.setTime(date.getTime() + (60*60*1000));
document.cookie = mycookie + ";expires=" + date.toGMTString();
```

This expiration date also provides a means for deleting cookies. This is done by re-creating the same cookie with an old expiration date—in this example, one day in the past.

```
var name = "cookie1";
var date = new Date();
date.setDate(date.getDate() - 1);
document.cookie = name + '=;expires=' + date.toGMTString();
```

Note that only the name of the cookie is needed to identify which cookie is to be overwritten. The value part is therefore left blank.

Path and Domain

In order to access a cookie, the document must be in the same domain and have the same path as specified by the cookie. By default the path is the location of the folder containing the document that created the cookie. The following example illustrates how to make the cookie visible to all paths in a given domain.

```
var mycookie = "cookie1=first";
var path = "path=/";
document.cookie = mycookie + ";" + path;
```

The domain defaults to the host part of the document's location, such as www.example.com. To make the cookie available to other subdomains of this domain, the www part can be left out, as in the following example.

```
var domain = "domain=.example.com";
document.cookie = mycookie + ";" +  domain + ";" + path;
```

The domain, path, and expires options may appear in any order. Keep in mind that it is not possible to retrieve these optional parameters from a cookie once they have been set.

CHAPTER 13

■ ■ ■

Error Handling

An error is a mistake in the code that the developer needs to fix or handle. For instance, the following line of code triggers a syntax error because of a missing parenthesis.

```
console.log("Hi";
```

When an error is encountered, the browser halts execution of the script. Most browsers do not inform the user when an error occurs. Instead, information about the error can be found in the browser's developer console. This information includes the filename, line number, and a description of the error, as the one seen below.

```
SyntaxError: missing ) after argument list
```

While syntax errors are easy to find and resolve, other errors can be harder to discover as they may only occur in certain situations. Furthermore, some errors may happen for reasons beyond the developer's control. For instance, a function may be unavailable if it is defined by an external file and that file fails to load. This triggers a reference error.

```
// Uncaught ReferenceError: missingFunc is not defined
missingFunc();
```

One way to prevent the execution of the script from halting is to check that the function exists before calling it, which can be done in the following manner.

```
if (typeof missingFunc === "function") {
    missingFunc(); // safe to use function
}
```

Suppose this error occurs in a function and that the function cannot continue as a result. The function then needs to signal its caller that it has failed. This is typically done by returning null or an error code from the function.

```
function foo() {
  if (typeof missingFunc === "function") {
      missingFunc(); // safe to use function
  }
  else { return null; }
}
```

This is often the best way for a function to handle an error, or exception, as the caller typically has the context necessary for deciding how to respond to the exception. However, sometimes there may be multiple stacked function calls that make this approach more cumbersome. As each function returns to its caller, the context of the exception is gradually lost, and the last function that gets a null value returned does not have any idea of what went wrong. To solve this JavaScript provides the try-catch statement.

Try-Catch

The try-catch statement consists of a try block containing the code that may cause an exception, and a catch clause for handling it. If the try block executes successfully the program will continue running after the try-catch statement, but if an exception occurs, execution will then be passed to the catch block.

```
try {
  missingFunc();
}
catch(e) {}
```

With this statement, exception handling code is only necessary at the point that knows how to handle the error. The functions in between the error and the exception handler do not need to concern themselves with the exception.

Catch Block

The catch clause defines an exception object. This object can be used to obtain more information about the exception, such as a description of the exception from the message property.

```
catch(e) {
  // "missingFunc is not defined"
  console.log(e.message);
}
```

Note that JavaScript does not provide a direct way for selectively catching exceptions. All potential exceptions need to be handled in the same catch block. Also keep in mind that syntax errors cannot be caught.

Finally

As the last clause in the try-catch statement, a finally block can be added. This block is used to clean up resources allocated in the try block and will always execute whether there is an exception or not.

```
try {
  missingFunc();
}
catch(e) { }
finally {
  console.log("Always executed");
}
```

Throwing Exceptions

User-defined exceptions can be generated with the throw statement. When this statement is reached, the function stops executing and the exception propagates up the caller stack until it is caught by a try-catch statement, or else handled by the browser.

```
function bar()
{
  if (typeof missingFunc === "function") {
      missingFunc();
  }
  else { throw new Error("missingFunc(): Function missing"); }
}
```

The throw keyword can be followed by whatever it is the function wants to signal. In this example, the Error constructor is used to create an exception value. This standard type is often used for creating user-defined exceptions. It takes a description of the error as a string argument. This argument is available through the error object's message property.

```
try {
  bar();
}
catch(e) {
  // "missingFunc(): Function missing"
  console.error(e.message);
}
```

Error objects also contain a name property. This property has the value "Error" for objects created with the Error constructor.

```
console.error(e.name); // "Error"
```

To make it easier to identify exceptions it can be preferable to throw custom error objects. This is especially useful when the code in the try clause can throw more than one type of exception. In the following code sample, an object literal is thrown with customized name and message properties. The name property can be examined in the catch clause to determine how the exception should be handled.

```
throw {
  name: 'CustomError',
  message: 'Error description'
}
```

CHAPTER 14

Ajax

Asynchronous JavaScript and XML, or Ajax, is a methodology for exchanging data with the server in the background, without having to do a full page refresh. This allows elements of a page to be updated based on user events, without disrupting what the user is doing on the page, thereby enabling the development of highly responsive web applications.

Exchanging Data

An Ajax request is made using the XMLHttpRequest object. The first step to making a request is to create an instance of this object.

```
var myRequest = new XMLHttpRequest();
```

To handle the server's response, an event handler is attached to the onload event of this object. The response is retrieved here with the responseText property and displayed in the console.

```
myRequest.addEventListener('load', myHandler);
function myHandler() {
  console.log(this.responseText);
}
```

The request is initialized using the object's open method, which is called with three arguments: the retrieval method, the URL, and a Boolean value. The retrieval method is commonly either "GET" or "POST." The "GET" method is typically used when fetching data and "POST" when sending data. The URL location is where the server data is available. This can be any text file, such as an HTML or XML document, or a server-side script that generates a text response. The last argument specifies if the request will be processed asynchronously, which is generally preferred, or if the send method should wait until the response is received.

```
var url = "mytext.txt";
myRequest.open("GET", url, true);
```

With the request ready it can now be sent using the send method. If information is to be submitted to a script on the server, this data is specified as an argument to the send method.

```
myRequest.send();
```

To follow along and test this Ajax request, you can place a text file called mytext.txt with some sample text in the same folder as your web document. Bear in mind that Ajax is subject to the same-origin policy of JavaScript, which means the specified location must be on the same server from where the script is loaded.

Server Response

When the server response is received, the HTTP status code should be checked to make sure the request was successful. The status code is available through the status property, and a successful request is indicated by the number 200. Other status codes signal a problem with the response, such as 404, which means the file was not found.

```
function myHandler() {
  if (this.status === 200)
    console.log(this.responseText);
}
```

The response is retrieved here using the responseText property, which returns the response as a text string. If the response is XML data instead, it can be retrieved as an XML object using the responseXML property. Such an object can be traversed using the standard DOM methods.

Ajax Event

The state of an Ajax request can be retrieved from the readyState property of the XMLHttpRequest object. This state is represented as a number from 0 to 4, where the response is fully received when the state reaches 4. A function can be attached to the onreadystatechange property to respond to each state change event. This can be used to update the user on the progress of the request.

```
myRequest.onreadystatechange = stateObserver;
function stateObserver() {
  switch(this.readyState) {
    case 0: console.log("Request not sent"); break;
    case 1: console.log("Request sent"); break;
    case 2: console.log("Response header received"); break;
    case 3: console.log("Downloading data"); break;
    case 4: console.log("Response data received"); break;
  }
}
```

CHAPTER 15

jQuery

The jQuery framework is a widely used JavaScript library designed to simplify DOM manipulation and eliminate browser incompatibilities.

Including jQuery

To include jQuery you can place the following reference in the <head> section of your web document. This loads the latest version of jQuery from Google's Hosted Libraries service, which at the time of writing is version 1.11.3.

```
<script src="https://ajax.googleapis.com/ajax/libs/jquery/1.11.3/jquery.min.
js"></script>
```

If you prefer to have a local copy of the script file, it can be obtained from jquery.com. However, linking to jQuery from a content delivery network (CDN), such as the link above, offers performance benefits. The CDN servers hosting jQuery are spread globally, reducing latency, and visitors who already have a cached copy from the same source will not have to download it again.

Using jQuery

When the jQuery script is included, it adds a single object named jQuery to the global namespace. This object provides access to the utility methods of the jQuery framework. Many of these methods are aimed at simplifying highly used JavaScript functionality, such as the isArray, isPlainObject, and isFunction methods, which provide easy ways to check if the passed argument is of one of these types.

```
jQuery.isArray( [1, 2] ); // true
jQuery.isPlainObject( {} ); // true
jQuery.isFunction( function() {} ); // true
```

The jQuery object is typically referenced through its dollar sign ($) alias, because it is shorter to type and brevity is a key feature of jQuery. The jQuery methods can therefore be called with an even shorter syntax. Here the type method is used, which returns the type of its argument as a string.

```
$.type(null); // "null"
$.type( [1, 2] ); // "array"
```

In instances such as these, the type method is more specific than the typeof operator.

```
typeof( null ); // "object"
typeof( [1, 2] ); // "object"
```

Element Selection

Access to and manipulation of DOM elements requires that the target elements are first selected, a process which jQuery greatly simplifies. Suppose a web document contains the following element that we want to select.

```
<p id="myid">My paragraph</p>
```

The jQuery object can be used as a function, which takes a single argument and returns a jQuery collection. If the argument is a CSS selector, the object returns a collection containing any DOM elements that match that selector. This provides a convenient way to select the paragraph.

```
var selection = $("#myid");
```

Compare this with the more verbose DOM method for selecting elements by their id.

```
var domNode = document.getElementById("myid");
```

An important difference between these selection methods is that the DOM method returns a reference to the DOM element, whereas the jQuery method returns a jQuery collection. The collection acts as a wrapper around the underlying DOM elements, providing easier-to-use methods for performing actions on those elements. If you want to use native DOM methods, the jQuery collection can be unwrapped to a raw DOM node using either the square bracket notation or the get method.

```
domNode = selection[0];
domNode = selection.get(0);
```

Conversely, a DOM element can be wrapped into a jQuery collection by passing it to the jQuery object.

```
var selection = $(domNode);
```

A jQuery collection is like an array that contains zero or more DOM elements. If no elements match the provided selector, or if no selector is provided, the returned collection is empty.

```
var empty = $();
```

The number of elements selected can be retrieved using the length property. In this case the length of the collection is zero.

```
console.log(empty.length); // "0"
```

If the selector matches more than one element, the returned collection will contain all matched elements. Consider the following div elements.

```
<div class="myclass" id="div1">First</div>
<div class="myclass" id="div2">Second</div>
```

Selecting these elements by their class name returns a collection with two elements.

```
var divs = $(".myclass");
console.log(divs.length); // "2"
```

A new selection can be added to a collection using the add method.

```
var div1 = $("#div1");
divs = div1.add("#div2");
```

Likewise, the not method takes one or more matched elements out of a collection.

```
var div2 = divs.not("#div1");
```

It is interesting to note that jQuery method calls are chainable, as they all return jQuery collections. The following line adds all div elements to an empty collection, and then removes the div2 element, leaving only the div1 element remaining.

```
var div1 = $().add("div").not("#div2");
```

Collection Traversal

Once selected, a collection can be manipulated through the methods of that collection object. To illustrate, the list below containing three list items will be used.

```
<ul id="mylist">
  <li>Item 1</li>
  <li>Item 2</li>
  <li>Item 3</li>
</ul>
```

The following query matches these list items and returns them as a collection.

```
var items = $("#mylist li");
```

This items collection now contains three jQuery elements. To extract a single element from this collection the eq method can be used with the element's index as its argument.

```
var first = items.eq(0);
var second = items.eq(1);
```

Providing a negative argument retrieves an element counted from the end of the collection instead.

```
var third = items.eq(-1);
```

Shortcut methods are available for retrieving the first or last element of a collection.

```
first = items.first();
third = items.last();
```

Alternatively, these method names can be used as suffixes when selecting the elements.

```
first = $("#mylist li:first");
second = $("#mylist li:eq(1)");
third = $("#mylist li:last");
```

There are several other index-related selectors, or filters, that allow for very precise selection queries. For example, the odd, even, lt (less than) and gt (greater than) filters.

```
var first_third = $("#mylist li:even");
second = $("#mylist li:odd");
first = $("#mylist li:lt(1)");
third = $("#mylist li:gt(1)");
```

DOM Traversal

The DOM tree can be traversed relative to elements in a collection. Using the previous list example, the second list item here is selected as a starting point.

```
var second = $("#mylist li:eq(1)");
```

From this element the DOM can be navigated sideways to sibling elements using the next and prev methods.

```
var third = second.next();
var first = second.prev();
```

To move up in the hierarchy the parent method is provided. In this case the unordered list element is selected.

```
var list = second.parent();
```

The children method can be used for moving downwards in the tree. It here returns all three list items as a collection.

```
var items = list.children();
```

To select all siblings of an element, the siblings method is available. Bear in mind that the original element is not included among the siblings.

```
var first_third = second.siblings();
```

If a collection contains more than one element, most collection methods affect all elements in the set. For instance, calling next on a collection consisting of the first and second list elements will return a collection containing the second and last list elements.

```
var first_second = $("#mylist li:lt(2)");
var second_third = first_second.next();
```

Modifying Attributes

The attr method is provided to access and modify the attributes of the selected elements. To illustrate, consider the following HTML.

```
<p id="myid" class="myclass">First paragraph</p>
<p class="myclass">Second paragraph</p>
```

When called with an attribute name, the attr method retrieves the current value of that attribute. If the collection contains more than one element, as in this case, only the attribute value for the first element in the set is retrieved.

```
$(".myclass").attr("id"); // "myid"
```

65

To add or change the value of an attribute, the name of that attribute and its new value is passed to the method. Since this collection contains two elements, both of them will be assigned the new attribute value.

```
$(".myclass").attr("title", "mytitle");
```

More than one attribute can be set at the same time by passing an object to the method consisting of attribute–value pairs.

```
$(".myclass").attr({
  lang: "en",
  dir: "rtl"
});
```

Attributes can be removed using the removeAttr method. If applied to a selection of multiple elements, each element will have that attribute removed.

```
$(".myclass").removeAttr("lang");
```

The css method allows CSS styles to be retrieved or changed through the style attribute of the element. In the following example the first paragraph is colored red.

```
$("#myid").css("color", "red");
```

Passing a single argument to the method retrieves the value of that style property from the style attribute, or undefined if the property has not been set.

```
$("#myid").css("color"); // "rgb(255, 0, 0)"
```

To change the style of an element it is preferable to apply classes that define these styles in external stylesheets, rather than to modify the style attribute. The addClass and removeClass methods provide a convenient way to do this, by allowing classes to be added or removed from the class attribute. Both methods take a single argument, which is a string specifying one or more classes to be added or removed.

```
$("#myid").addClass("class1 class2");
$("#myid").removeClass("class2");
$("#myid").attr("class"); // "myclass class1"
```

The hasClass method determines whether any matched elements are assigned the specified class. Given the previous HTML, the following code returns true.

```
$("#myid").hasClass("myclass"); // true
```

Creating Elements

Besides manipulating existing DOM nodes, the jQuery object can also be used to create new elements by passing HTML markup to it in the form of a string argument. The string must consist of a single top-level HTML element, but this element may contain any number of child nodes.

```
var myDiv = $("<div>My container</div>");
```

Two methods are provided by jQuery for modifying the content of an element: text and html. The html method changes the content of the element to the given string.

```
myDiv = myDiv.html("<b>Hello HTML</b>");
```

Calling the method without an argument retrieves the HTML content of that element. If the collection contains more than one element, only the markup of the first element is returned.

```
// "<b>Hello HTML</b>"
console.log(myDiv.html());
```

In contrast, invoking the text method without an argument retrieves the content of the element stripped of any HTML tags.

```
// "Hello HTML"
console.log(myDiv.text());
```

Likewise, when given an argument the text method will escape any HTML in the string and insert it in the element as plain text content.

```
myDiv.text("<b>Hello text</b>");

// &lt;b&gt;Hello text&lt;/b&gt;
console.log(myDiv.html());
```

Keep in mind that newly created elements are not automatically included in the DOM. They exist only as part of their respective jQuery collection.

Moving Elements

An element can be moved around or inserted into the DOM tree using one of the jQuery insertion methods. To illustrate, take the following two elements.

```
<div id="content">My content</div>
<div id="container"></div>
```

The append method takes an element as its argument and adds it to the end of each element of a jQuery collection. In this example, the content element is selected and moved into the container element as the last child.

```
$("#container").append($("#content"));
```

To insert the element as the first child, use the prepend method instead.

```
$("#container").prepend($("<div>First child</div>"));
```

The after method places the element immediately before the collection as a sibling.

```
$("#container").after($("<div>After</div>"));
```

The before method works the same way, but adds its argument before the collection as a sibling.

```
$("#container").before($("<div>Before</div>"));
```

Upon executing these lines of code the HTML is transformed into the markup shown below.

```
<div>Before</div>
<div id="container">
  <div>First child</div>
  <div id="content">My content</div>
</div>
<div>After</div>
```

Ready Method

In most cases, the appropriate time to run scripts is when the web document has been loaded and the full DOM hierarchy is available. For this purpose, jQuery provides the ready method, which takes as its argument a function to be executed upon this event.

```
function myHandler(e) { console.log("DOM ready"); }
$(document).ready(myHandler);
```

The document selector may be omitted since the ready method can only be called in the context of the document.

```
$(myHandler); // alternative syntax
```

Bear in mind that the jQuery ready event is different from the DOM load event, which does not trigger until all external resources, such as images, have been fully loaded.

Event Handling

Event handling is simplified with jQuery's on method. This method attaches an event handler for an event to the selected elements. To give an example, consider the following list.

```
<ul id="mylist">
  <li>Item 1</li>
  <li>Item 2</li>
</ul>
```

A click event for these list items can be registered in a single step with the following code.

```
$("#mylist li").on("click", myListHandler);
```

The event handler below uses the this selector to retrieve a reference to the element where the event occurs, so clicking for instance the first list item will display "Item 1" in the console.

```
function myListHandler(e) {
  console.log( $(this).text() );
}
```

There are shorthand methods for some events, such as click, change, keypress, blur, and focus. This provides an alternative syntax for the previous example of registering an event handler.

```
$("#mylist li").click(myListHandler);
```

Adding event handlers through jQuery provides the same benefits as the W3C method of registering events, allowing multiple event handlers to be attached for the same element and event. It also has the added benefit of being cross-browser compatible with IE6-8, unlike the W3C method, both in terms of registering the event successfully and in passing the correct event object.

Ajax

The steps to using Ajax is greatly simplified with jQuery, to the point of requiring only a single method for the whole process of initializing, sending, and receiving a server request. The same example used in Chapter 14 to display the content of a text file from the server is seen here using jQuery.

```
$.ajax({
  url: "mytext.txt",
  type: "GET",
  async: "true",
  success: function(data) {
    console.log(data);
  }
});
```

The success method specified here gets called if the Ajax request succeeds. Only the url property must be set for the ajax method. Other properties are optional and can be left unspecified to use their default values. In this case, the type and async properties are both using their default values, so they do not need to be specified.

```
$.ajax({
  url: "mytext.txt",
  success: function(data) {
    console.log(data);
  }
});
```

There is another, shorter way to accomplish this same task by using the get method. This method requests server data using an HTTP GET request. It takes two arguments – the URL and the callback function – to be executed if the request succeeds.

```
$.get("mytext.txt", function(data, status) {
  console.log(data);
});
```

Similar to the get method, there is also a post method that sends a server request using an HTTP POST request. This method includes an extra argument containing the data to be sent along to the server.

```
$.post("myscript.php", {
    name: "Alex",
    age: "25"
  }, function(data, status) {
  console.log(data);
});
```

The jQuery methods of sending Ajax requests automatically adds backward compatibility for IE<7. Specifically, the ajax method takes into consideration that IE5-6 does not have the XMLHttpRequest object and instead uses an ActiveX object.

Index

Get the eBook for only $5!

Why limit yourself?

Now you can take the weightless companion with you wherever you go and access your content on your PC, phone, tablet, or reader.

Since you've purchased this print book, we're happy to offer you the eBook in all 3 formats for just $5.

Convenient and fully searchable, the PDF version enables you to easily find and copy code—or perform examples by quickly toggling between instructions and applications. The MOBI format is ideal for your Kindle, while the ePUB can be utilized on a variety of mobile devices.

To learn more, go to www.apress.com/companion or contact support@apress.com.

Printed in the United States
By Bookmasters